AF176493

One Seeing
One Knowing
One Love

Andreas Müller

on Master Eckhart

Impressum

Bibliografische Information der Deutschen Nationalbibliothek: Die Deutsche Nationalbibliothek verzeichnet diese Publikation in der Deutschen Nationalbibliografie; detaillierte bibliografische Daten sind im Internet über www.dnb.de abrufbar.

Herstellung und Verlag:
BoD – Books on Demand, Norderstedt

ISBN: 9783755781233

Contents

This sermon

"If anyone cannot understand this sermon, he need not worry. For so long as a man is not equal to this truth, he cannot understand my words, for this is a naked truth which has come direct from the heart of God."[1]

~

This message is an impersonal message. It doesn't belong to anyone. It doesn't speak to anyone. It is direct. It means what it says and still remains empty. It doesn't contain a method. There is nothing in it that can be recognized.

I know that with Master Eckhart it always sounds as if there is something to be found. Again and again, it sounds as if there is someone who could be in the right way. What Eckhart meant remains speculation. Yet some of his words seem to resonate with me.

Nevertheless – there was no Master Eckhart, just as there is no such thing as me or any separate authority. These words have no meaning. There is no need to work on them or cling to them.
They are like a song, and whoever hears it may feel joy. If you don't hear it, don't be bothered by it.

There is nothing to be found and nothing to lose. What appears to be happening is naturally everything. That is the joy – a joy that nobody owns and that is everything at the same time. That is what these words speak of. And yet they add nothing.

Master Eckhart

Q: You wanted to write a book about Master Eckhart ...

A: ... or at least say something about him.

Q: So what happened?

A: This little book. The beginning was difficult. I had a look at the "Sermons and Tracts." And then I noticed: Everything is already there as it should be!
The passages that I wanted to comment on were and are so clear that there is not much left to comment on. And then it just happened.
It is amazing what this Dominican monk said back then without having had any serious problems.

Q: Wasn't he brought to trial?

A: At the end of his life, yes, or even a little later. In fact, it went well for a long time. And it's amazing that he was only charged for 28 sentences. Posthumously. Because he died before he was sentenced.

Q: What is he saying so bluntly?

A: For example: that there is no one. And that God is more of a non-God. And that existence is more like non-existence.

Q: That the Church couldn't fully agree with this is perhaps understandable. But do you agree?

A: At least such sentences can be transferred to my reading. For example: There is no observable reality. We live in absolute blind flight, just like the entire apparent universe.

This is because the observer himself is illusory. Even speaking of an observer who exists in some way – real, unreal, illusory – can give the impression that such a thing exists.

But there is no such thing. There is no one. There is no observer. There is no separate awareness.

And because awareness is not real, what is being witnessed cannot really be witnessed either! What is, is absolutely blind to itself.

Q: You mean that's what Eckhart meant when he said existence is more like non-existence?

A: Yes, the seemingly everyday experience of presence has no substance.

Q: Do I have to understand that? Or may I agree with Eckhart: If anyone cannot understand this sermon, he need not worry.

A: Nobody can really talk about it. In order for it to appear to be reported, this apparent illusion must dissolve.

I know someone who has searched spiritually all his life. He has learned a lot and has spent the past few years experiencing awareness. This seemed to be all he had after his long search.

Then he tried to combine that awareness experience with this non-dual message. He assumed that I, too, had recognized the awareness experience as the "natural reality" and that I was trying to convey it in my own words.

And then, suddenly and unexpectedly, the awareness was gone, too. Zack, boom, just like that.

It wasn't a big deal, nor was it a big change. But only then did the search end. The search was not satisfied, nor was there an experience of arrival. Rather, the experience of awareness or presence turned out to be non-existent.

I can neither explain it, nor does it sound logical. When it fizzles out, it just fizzles out. Then nothing else can be reported.

Q: Eckhart can't explain any of this either ...

A: Eckhart can't explain and I can't explain that there is nothing to explain.

It is impossible to explain to the presence that the experience of presence is not real. Conversely, in order to explain a real circumstance, one would need a real presence. That goes in circles.

The absence of 'I am' is not a new fact to be aware of. That is the crux: There is nobody who knows, who experiences, who could confirm or deny. There is no explanation for anything.

And that is freedom. *As long as you do not equal this truth, you will not understand this speech.*

Q: Kiss my ass!

Do not seek anything

"Those who seek nothing, neither honor nor profit nor inwardness nor holiness nor reward nor heaven, but who have renounced all this, including what is their own – in such men God is glorified."[2]

~

Q: Don't strive for anything, forego everything ... Who should do that?

A: Nobody. It is impossible. But liberation is the end of the seeker and at the same time the end of the search. Liberation is not the result of renunciation or *seeking*, it is not the successful ending of the search.

Liberation is the seeker's apparent collapse into the surprising obviousness that no one exists.

Renouncing all this is the end of the search itself. It is not only the end of the search in so-called material things, but also the end of the search for spiritual goals.

Devotion, enlightenment, liberation, absorption in God – behind all these goals lies egocentricity. That is nothing but self-exaggeration in the hope of giving up your own existence and thereby becoming one with God.

Q: And in whom is God glorified, *as Eckhart puts it?*

A: In nobody. *To be glorified in God* means that perfection is the natural reality. This natural reality is neither discovered nor achieved. It is neither experienced nor not experienced. It is what remains when the experiencer turns out to be non-existent.

Suffer God

"Now if, with this power, the soul sees anything imaged, whether she sees the image of an angel or her own image, it is an imperfection in her. If she sees God as He is God, or as He is an image, or as He is three, it is an imperfection in her. But when all images are detached from the soul and she sees nothing but the one alone, then the naked essence of the soul finds the naked, formless essence of divine unity, which is superessential being, passive, reposing in itself. Oh wonder of wonders, what noble suffering that is, that the essence of the soul can suffer nothing but the bare unity of God!"[3]

~

Q: When all images of the soul are detached ...

A: Yes, this is what I call liberation: the end of the illusion that there is such a thing as a detached or separate person. The *naked, formless essence of divine unity* – that means: This freedom cannot be experienced mentally, emotionally or energetically – *formless*. Such liberation is closer than any experience.

However, what can result from it, *when all images of the soul are detached*, is an apparent mental and emotional liberation within the personal story. Because many thoughts and emotional patterns, neuroses and trauma seem to be related to the experience of being a separate person.

As a story, one could say that there is such a thing as an interaction between the experience of being a person and the arising of thoughts and emotions.

If the illusion of separation evaporates, in the words of Eckhart: *when the soul sees nothing but the one alone*, then something like a liberation process begins within the story, which gradually washes out all mental and emotional obligations.

However, this apparent process is not the point.

The – apparent! – crucial point is actually whether the illusion of (self-)experience is what is apparently happening or not. Everything else is simply a symptom of this experience.

Q: What would such symptoms be?

A: An apparent symptom of separation would be living in stories and in searching. It is a complete dream world; an apparent energetic rotation within this assumption of being a person and a circling around the artificial problems the artificial person believes it has.

The main problem of the person is the search for lasting personal fulfillment. However, it is a problem that can never be solved, because there is no person and no state of personal fulfillment.

Q: And is that what Master Eckhart is talking about?

A: Yes, to me it looks as if Master Eckhart describes this apparent liberation – and works out in many texts what this liberation is or what it is not. In this respect, he does a natural *neti neti*, which corresponds exactly to this, "my" message.

Q: Are there any signs or symptoms of liberation?

A: Ultimately, all symptoms relate to the breakdown of the artificial structures of the 'I' experience. The collapse of mental and emotional structures would be such an example.

Q: The breakdown of mental and emotional structures sounds unpleasant.

A: It is the breakdown of any idea of psychology. Psychology turns out to be the scientific counterpart to spirituality: Both start from an inner core or a true center. In spirituality it would be either the soul or something like pure awareness, while in psychology there is the assumption of a real 'I' inherent in the body.

The whole psycho-mental and psycho-emotional structure revolves around this experience that there is 'someone.' If this inner core turns out to be an illusion (in Eckhart's words: *when all images of the soul are detached*), the whole structure, which seems to revolve around this core, gradually turns out to be an illusion. It fades or falls off – in parts or completely.

Or maybe it will just be a softening of the structure. In any case, I have the impression that I can perceive it that way both with myself and with everyone I would describe as "apparently liberated." What remains, in Eckhart's words, is *naked, formless essence*.

Q: Occasionally you claim that these are all just stories?

A: Oh, yes, there is neither me nor people I could recognize as liberated. There is neither a psychological structure nor a softening of it. None of this is real or significant.

Q: Well, which one is it?

A: Nothing matters. Everything remains without consequences. What appears to be happening is everything.

Q: Master Eckhart says that if the soul sees God, ... it is an imperfection in her.

A: He describes that all looking is "illusory," that every experience of awareness is connected with an experience of imperfection. Both the finest self-experience – *the soul that sees its own image* – and an experience of unity or God – *the soul that sees God* – are personal experiences and therefore accompanied by a feeling of lack.

Q: Could it be that he got away with such puzzles for so long because nobody understood them? What does it mean that the soul can only see nothing but the one alone *when all that is imagined is detached?*

A: If there is just looking, then that is what appears to be happening. There is not really "something" that is seen there. Then there is neither an image of what is looking nor of what is seen. *Then the naked essence of the soul finds the naked, formless essence of divine unity, which is superessential being, passive, reposing in itself.* Then everything is no-thing.

Of course, I wouldn't say that something is really found then! In the melting away of everything imagined – in the melting away of every self-experience – that which is turns out to be perfect. It turns out to be 'everything,' formless and unseparated. Of course, it turns out to be all of that while remaining exactly what it already is. The body, thoughts, feelings, the world, trees are formless and unseparated. However, for no one!

Q: Or is it for someone? Eckhart says that the soul, the only true unity of God, suffers?

A: When the illusion of self-awareness fizzles out, all that remains is the natural reality. It is neither found nor realized. It is just what appears to be happening.

"You" have virtually no chance, because there is nothing left than the bare "being no-thing." No-thing suffers itself, so to speak. It cannot find itself, it cannot escape, nor can it ever become anything else.

But: There is no thing that is no-thing. It's just what appears to be happening. The fact that we sit here and talk to one another is the natural, unknown, formless reality, which cannot be found, because it already is; which cannot be realized, because there is nothing that has the capability of an additional realization. Therefore, Master Eckhart could speak of "suffering."

Q: All right, I agree with this form of suffering.

A: Oh yes!

Leave yourself

*"Let man first leave himself,
then he leaves everything."*[4]

~

Q: Can you let yourself?

A: Spiritual seekers at least strive to do so. But there is
no one who can do that.

Q: So what does Eckhart mean by that?

A: He might be referring to the fact that all seeking is
useless as long as there is 'someone' who seeks.
As an exception, the opposite applies that for those
who have *left themselves* – or as I would put it: when it
turns out that there is no one – every search ends.
All questions are superfluous in the melting away of
the illusion that there is a real person.
Master Eckhart hits the nail on the head: Every search,
every question about the meaning of life, every
question about perfection, comes out of the experience
of being a separate entity.
As a story, one could say that one should first see
whether the person who seeks fulfillment even exists.

But the dilemma is that there is no one at all. Before the seeking begins, there is nothing that should or could be seeking. So the dilemma is that there is no dilemma.

Q: Let's leave that for now.

Aware of God

"Shall the soul become aware of God, she must also forget herself and lose herself. For as long as she sees and knows herself, she does not see God."[5]

~

A: As long as there is a sense of self – *seeing itself and knowing about itself* – apparent separation takes place.

Q: And then there is no awareness of God either?

A: There is no soul that can become aware of God. Therefore, the soul has to lose itself. It is the falling back of awareness into the unknown; the sinking of the experience of separation into absence.

Q: So what does shall the soul become aware of God *mean?*

A: Eckhart probably means liberation – the apparent obviousness that harmony is the natural reality. But: No one is aware of it. There is no experience of this harmony.

Q: No one, nobody, apparently, no-thing ...

A: When you talk to me there is an immediate answer. There is this report, which on the one hand is what is apparently happening. On the other hand, it does not come from a separate or real awareness.

A paraphrase of *the soul shall become aware of God* is that what is, reveals itself as what is. Apparently, because there is neither something recognized, nor is there any real awareness of it.

In that sense, awareness is blind to what appears to be happening. This obviousness is also apparent because nothing really becomes obvious. And yet: What we are talking about is undisguised because it is what appears to be happening.

Q: Should we give Master Eckhart a quick call and ask what he thinks about it?

A: We can try. But I suppose there is nobody.

How to love God?

'Then how should I love God?'

*You should love God nonspiritually: that is to say the soul
should be de-spirited, stripped of spiritual dress. For as long
as the soul is in spirit form, she has images; as long as she
has images, she has means; as long as she has means, she has
not unity or simplicity, and as long as she has not
simplicity she has never rightly loved God, for true love lies
in simplicity. Therefore your soul should be de-spirited of all
spirit, she should be spiritless, for if you love God as He is
God, as He is spirit, as He is person and as He is image – all
that must go!*

'Well, how should I love Him then?'

*You should love Him as He is: a non-God, a non-spirit, a
non-person, a non-image; rather, as He is a sheer pure
limpid One, detached from all duality. And in that One may
we eternally sink from nothingness to nothingness. So help
us God. Amen.[6]*

~

*Q: Sink into one, become one, yes, that's it, that's what it's
all about!*

A: You cannot become one because nobody is already
there. The experience of self – the experience of being

"spirit" – is illusory. It has no substance, which means "there is nobody there."

The apparent person is this self-experience. It experiences itself as 'something.' To experience yourself as 'something' is the seemingly experienced separation from God.

Then there seems to be something separate from what is apparently happening. Then there is 'I' and 'something else.' Then the world is seen from a separate point of view. One lives "in pictures," in seeing things.

Q: Yes, exactly, and that's why Eckhart's wording in that One may we eternally sink *sounds so promising!*

A: Yes, from the experience of separation the assumption arises that there is a way back to wholeness. The assumption is that there are steps and stages, methods and techniques.

As long as this self-experience seems to exist, one worships "things" – ideas and conceptions, a certain way of life, a priest, a guru, money or Buddha or Jesus on the cross.

The apparent person hopes that these things are mediators on the way to personal fulfillment.

That's the illusion. It is based on the experience that one is 'something' – a self that experiences itself and is aware of its presence. A self that has to find its way back to perfection.

What is being reported here is that there is no one.

Not only the ideas and conceptions in which the person lives are illusory, this whole experience has no substance. *Therefore your soul should be de-spirited of all spirit.*

Q: So when I stand there with no ideas or conceptions, I can become one.

A: You cannot become one. Love is the natural reality that can neither be achieved nor done. If the illusion that there is 'something' evaporates, the assumption that one is separate from love evaporates.
There is no god, no spirit, no person, no image to love. Love is the natural reality for no one.
That is the liberation that is already.

Glory is everywhere

"In every work, even evil, evil I say,
as of punishment and of sin,
the glory of God is manifested and reflects equally."[7]

~

Q: God reflects even in evil ...

A: There is neither "right" nor "wrong," there is neither something that is within oneness, nor is there something that is outside of oneness. There is no unity as such at all. What appears to be happening is naturally whole and coherent; beyond good or bad, right or wrong. This cannot be known or experienced. It is not a theory to be adopted – and yet it is an absolute surprise that what apparently happens is perfect in its apparent "being as it is."

Q: Why is "being as it is" also "apparent" now?

A: Because there is no such thing as a known or conscious "being as it is." How it is, is unknown because it is inexperienced. Nobody knows how what apparently happens really is. Therefore, there is no real "being as it is." What life, breathing, feeling, walking really is, is unknown. It just is what it is. Effortlessly.

Q: But thankfully, God's glory reflects in evil ...

A: There is no reason or explanation for it. Wholeness is the natural reality, which is causeless and uncreated. The natural reality is unconditional and without a cause. What apparently happens is not done by anything and unconditionally itself. That it is coherent is not the result of something. It is not whole because it is meaningful, good or sacred. Also, it is not whole because it leads to a goal. Wholeness or coherence is completely surprising and at the same time absolutely ordinary.

Q: No matter what comes up, you have to see it positively.

A: No, what we are talking about is not a concept. It is not an attempt to speak nicely or to cover it up with a sacred idea. What apparently happens does not need that at all. What apparently happens does not need to be transformed from something wrong into something that is right. It does not need an answer to be itself. Nothing can and nothing has to be made good. Pain does not need to be answered. Suffering does not need to be made good. "Goodness" is the natural reality.

Q: Okay, and this can allow to see things differently?

A: Yes, as soon as the search for an answer comes up. But the pain does not need an answer. It neither knows itself, nor does it have any ideas about itself. It is simply itself. Just like every flower, stone, animal, thought and feeling is itself. Even the apparent experience of separation is itself, even if the search for an answer and an arrival takes place within this experience. However: No one arrives, because there is no one on a path. No one has to arrive, because what apparently happens is blindly complete.

Q: That's all I need! "Blindly"!

A: Because there is no one who experiences it as perfect. Nobody who has to recognize it as perfect. Nobody who sees.

Q: You're telling me …

Needs and desires

"The other day I was pondering whether or not I would accept or desire anything from God. I wanted to consider this carefully as receiving from God, from a lower position would liken me to a servant. And in giving, God would resemble a master. It should not be so with eternal life."[8]

~

Q: Eckhart didn't want anything so as not to feel like a recipient of alms?

A: Desirelessness is the natural reality. Fulfilment, wholeness, peace is the natural reality.
What seems to happen is already without desire. It neither needs the absence of desires, nor does it need their fulfilment.

Q: Needlessness, frugality, renunciation, the ideal of the monks. Eckhart achieved it?

A: No, there is no one to reach this natural reality. Needs are what apparently happen.
I get caught looking for something to eat at the fridge at night. When hungry and tired, I become intolerable and the time in my company is not a pleasant one.

The need for harmony and sleep is just as much what apparently happens as going to the toilet.

But the hope and the longing to find real personal fulfilment in the apparent fulfillment of needs turns out to be illusory.

Q: But enlightenment or awakening is a kind of fulfillment.

A: No, it is not that the longing is fulfilled in the end of the "I-illusion" or that there is an experience of this fulfillment. Hope and longing for personal fulfillment just do not seem to happen anymore.

The search for personal fulfillment ends in the moment the apparent self turns out to be illusory.

Q: That's something!

A: Apparently! The experience of being separate from life, of being separate from freedom and wholeness - this experience disappears. The felt necessity to ask for something from life simply dissolves together with the illusion that someone is there at all.

There is no separation means: to be on a par with natural reality. There is no separation means that there is no one who has lost something. There is no separation means that there is no one to speak to God. According to Meister Eckhart: neither servant nor master. There is no hierarchy.

Q: I agree, I'll get there!

A: Neither you nor me nor anyone.

Not knowing

"But we say God is not a being and not intellectual and does not know this or that. Thus God is free of all things, and so He is all things. To be poor in spirit, a man must be poor of all his own knowledge: not knowing any thing, *not God, nor creature nor himself."*[9]

~

Q: Emptiness is form and form is emptiness, says the Heart Sutra attributed to Buddha. But nobody understands that.

A: What happens is real and unreal. It is free of all things and yet it is everything.

Q: Should anyone understand that?

A: No. To understand this is neither necessary nor possible. It describes the natural reality. It can neither be known nor experienced. There is no one who could do that.

Q: What's the point of the statement?

A: It does not have a point. It is not coming from anywhere. It is a direct sharing.

Q: Direct, so probably coming from what is called God?

A: There is no overarching reality that is "God." "God" is what appears to be happening. I sometimes speak of 'oneness,' but that doesn't really exist either. There is absolutely no statement to describe reality. The very assumption that there is a certain kind of reality comes from knowledge. "Emptiness is form and form is emptiness" does not know about itself. What apparently happens does not know about itself. It neither knows what it is, how it is, nor if it is. It just is. Apparently.

Q: Nobody knows anything ...

A: What appears to be happening is everything. There is nothing behind it, above or below it. There is nothing in it or anywhere else. Still, it's no-thing.

Q: At least ...

A: "No-thing" means "emptiness is form." And that means that God is free of all things and at the same time he is all things.

Q: Spiritual teachers occasionally advise to leave knowledge aside and to forego thinking.

A: That is not what is meant here. Many spiritual

teachers believe that personal history is what constitutes the illusory self. On the other hand, they see pure awareness as the real self. From such a perspective, it makes sense to try to not think.

However, that is already within knowledge. It is exactly the awareness experience which seems to know about its own existence. At least, that's what it thinks. But it is precisely this knowledge that is illusory. "I am aware of myself" is the illusion. "I am aware of myself" is the dream.

That is why Master Eckhart writes that one should know neither about oneself nor about God. All knowledge is illusory because all experience is illusory. God, or what appears to be happening, does not experience itself. Although it is itself, it does not know anything about itself.

All ideas about how one could find and know one's true self, that one could see or even experience God, are part of the dream. The idea that one can know and experience oneself as divine awareness is also an illusion. There is neither an "I" nor a God nor any kind of knowledge.

Q: I imagine not having to experience anything to be pretty relaxing.

A: How it is, is unimaginable. 'I am' means 'to experience.' The end of the separate reality is the end of the illusion of experience. There is no knowing in it. But since there is already no one, nothing is really known already now.

Q: If you say so. I feel differently.

A: This 'I' which thinks it knows itself and the world has no substance. This entire world of presence does not exist. The 'I' is already insubstantial. No one is there.

This something

"For all that ever came out of God, a pure activity is appointed. The proper work of man is to love and to know. Now the question is, Wherein does blessedness lie most of all? Some masters have said it lies in knowing, some say that it lies in loving: others say it lies in knowing and loving, and they say better. But we say it lies neither in knowing nor in loving: for there is something in the soul from which both knowledge and love flow: but it does not itself know or love in the way the powers of the soul do. Whoever knows this, knows the seat of blessedness. This has neither before nor after, nor is it expecting anything to come, for it can neither gain nor lose. And so it is deprived of the knowledge that God is at work in it: rather, it just is itself, enjoying itself God-fashion."[10]

~

Q: In Hindu spirituality there are two paths to liberation: love and devotion on the one hand and the path of knowledge on the other.

A: Yes, that's right, the Bhakti path is the path of devotion, the Jnani path is the path of knowledge. Sometimes both are also connected.

Q: Do you recommend it?

A: No, there is no path. It is the apparent person who thinks it is on a path. Both approaches are part of the dream. The assumption that one must tread a path back to God comes from the separate experience. Both methods play with the idea that they produce experiences that feel good.

In the practice of devotion there are impressive experiences of love and unity. They give the seeker the impression that they are on the right track. Part of the idea of liberation is the idea that it must be about the absolutely positive experience.

The same thing happens on the apparent path of knowledge. Every apparent realization is accompanied by the feeling of having achieved something. That reinforces the impression of making headway along the path.

All of this is part of the dream. When the illusion turns out to be an illusion, the experience of being separate fizzles out, and with it automatically the idea that a path and an approach are required. What is cannot be known, because it is no-thing.

What is cannot be loved, because it is love. Devotion and knowledge merge into the natural reality that is love and self-evident. The natural reality is exactly what appears to be happening.

Q: And what appears to be happening is perfect?

A: Yes, it is. It does not wait for anything, and it does not need anything. In that sense, it is naturally perfect. It never knows that something is missing. Therefore, it cannot search for anything. That which is, is blindly and blessedly itself. There can be no realization of it, because it is already so.

Q: But it sounds very promising when Master Eckhart writes that out of something in the soul flow both knowledge and love. *Obviously, there is something to experience after all?*

A: I don't know what he meant. But it could be a description of what happens in these talks: What is being referred to is the natural reality. Apparently, knowledge is communicated here, and love is also experienced. At the same time, however, love and knowledge do not know themselves and do not experience themselves as love and knowledge.

In (apparent) liberation, the energy seems to be reversed: While the seeker energy constantly needs something and wants to devour or possess everything – love and knowledge, for example – this energetic dynamic seems to cease in liberation. The energy even begins to flow away. That could be what he means when he says that *knowledge and love flow out,* but they *do not themselves know or love.* Since nothing is separate anymore, only the natural reality remains.

Q: He writes: Whoever knows this, knows the seat of

blessedness.

A: Nobody can and will get to know this blessedness. There is no path to it and no person who arrives in this blessedness. Nonetheless, the natural reality is that in which the experience of love and the experience of knowledge coincide. It is the end of the illusion that there is an experiencer.

Q: *There is no experiencer ... is there at least experience?*

A: I wouldn't put it that way. For me, the process of experiencing and something that experiences belong together. Even if the person is determined to view experience as impersonal, it remains an experienced reality; something that actually seems to be happening. From the point of view of the apparent person, this makes sense because to experience is their reality. The experience is apparently known and lived.

Q: *But in reality, there is no experience?*

A: There is no experience.

Q: *But are there thoughts and feelings? Or maybe not?*

A: Apparently there are. Apparently, the body "experiences" thoughts and feelings. The body doesn't really experience them, it just lives. In doing so, it thinks, feels, sees, hears, smells, walks and stands, but it does not experience it from a separate point of view. This is what I mean when I say that there is no experience.

Q: I see myself as having experiences!

A: To experience yourself as experiencing is illusory.

Q: Because I don't exist and nobody else?

A: Yes, exactly. There is nothing that experiences.

Q: Then there is probably nothing that can be experienced …

A: Yes, there is no known or experienced reality.

Q: Then there was probably never a Master Eckhart either …

A: And yet, or precisely because of that, he was prosecuted and persecuted …

One seeing, one knowing, one love

*"The man who abides in the will of God wills nothing else
than what God is, and what He wills. If he were ill he would
not wish to be well. If he really abides in God's will, all pain
is to him a joy, all complication, simple: yea, even the pains
of hell would be a joy to him. He is free and gone out from
himself, and from all that he receives, he must be free. If my
eye is to discern colour, it must itself be free from all
colour. The eye with which I see God is the same with which
God sees me. My eye and God's eye is one eye, and
one sight, and one knowledge, and one love."*[11]

~

The surprise is that it is all whole and complete. It does
not have to be good or pleasant, however, everything
has its own unknowable taste of completion and
harmony.

Of course, this harmony is for no one, as oneself is the
very wholeness that's being spoken of here. Nothing
gives or adds or improves anything – it is all "this"
already.

That there is nothing different from what God is
means that there is nothing outside of this wholeness.
Everything (literally everything!) is itself – undivided,
singular, unbound, whole and complete. Already.

About Master Eckhart

Master Eckhart (also Eckehart, Eckhart von Hochheim; * around 1260 in Hochheim or in Tambach; † before April 30, 1328 in Avignon) was an influential Thuringian theologian and philosopher of the late Middle Ages.

His unconventional, sometimes provocatively worded statements and his sharp contradiction to the beliefs widespread at the time caused a stir. After many years in the service of the order, Eckhart was denounced and charged with heresy (false doctrine, deviation from orthodoxy) only in the last years of his life. Eckhart died before the proceedings against him were concluded. Subjecting himself to the Pope's judgment from the outset, he escaped classification as a heretic, but Pope John XXII condemned some of his statements as false doctrines and forbade the circulation of the works containing them. Nevertheless, Eckhart's ideas had a considerable influence on late medieval spirituality in the German and Dutch regions.[12]

1   O'C Walshe, Maurice (2009): The Complete Mystical Works of Meister Eckhart. Pearl River, NY: Herder & Herder, The Crossroad Publishing Company, p. 425, emphasis in original. URL: https://philocyclevl.files.wordpress.com/2016/10/meister-eckhart-maurice-o-c-walshe-bernard-mcginn-the-complete-mystical-works-of-meister-eckhart-the-crossroad-publishing-company-2009.pdf (12/19/2021).

2   Ibid, p. 26.

3   Ibid, p. 462.

4   Aphorismen.de – Aphorismen, Zitate, Sprüche und Gedichte, URL: https://www.aphorismen.de/zitat/16008 (05/01/2021), translated by Andreas Müller.

5   Aphorismen.de – Aphorismen, Zitate, Sprüche und Gedichte, URL: https://www.aphorismen.de/zitat/64091 (05/01/2021), translated by Andreas Müller.

6   O'C Walshe, Maurice (2009): The Complete Mystical Works of Meister Eckhart. Pearl River, NY: Herder & Herder, The Crossroad Publishing Company, p. 464–465. URL: https://philocyclevl.files.wordpress.com/2016/10/meister-eckhart-maurice-o-c-walshe-bernard-mcginn-the-complete-mystical-works-of-meister-eckhart-the-crossroad-publishing-company-2009.pdf (12/19/2021).

7 Quint, Josef [Hrsg.] (1979): Meister Eckehart: Zürich: Diogenes, S. 450, translated by Andreas Müller.

8 Quint, Josef [Hrsg]: Meister Eckehart, 1979. S. 451. translated by Andreas Müller

9   O'C Walshe, Maurice (2009): The Complete Mystical Works of Meister Eckhart. Pearl River, NY: Herder & Herder, The Crossroad Publishing Company, p. 423, emphasis in original. URL: https://philocyclevl.files.wordpress.com/2016/10/meister-eckhart-maurice-o-c-walshe-bernard-mcginn-the-complete-mystical-works-of-meister-eckhart-the-crossroad-publishing-

company-2009.pdf. (12/19/2021).

10   Ibid, p. 422.
11   Wikipuote, URL https://en.wikiquote.org/wiki/Meister_Eckhart
12 Meister Eckhart, Wikipedia article (excerpt), URL:
https://de.wikipedia.org/wiki/Meister_Eckhart (05/01/2021),
translated by Andreas Müller.

About Andreas Müller

Andreas was born in 1979 in Ludwigsburg in Southern
Germany. After years of seeking in spirituality,
he met Tony Parsons in 2009.
"First, I was shocked. Though I had already known
and experienced a lot, this was something new and
unexpected. Suddenly, for no reason, I heard what
Tony was saying, and soon it was undeniable:
There is no one."
Since 2011, Andreas has been holding talks and
intensives throughout the world.

www.thetimelesswonder.com

Acknowledgements

Master Eckhart

Nadine Reichmann

Dietmar Bittrich

Dorothea Gruß

Benoît Strauss

Ieva Gaidulis

Tony & Claire Parsons

My family